Traffic Light Lines

TRAFFIC LIGHT LINES

A Simplified Handwriting Program

KIMBERLY LANE, OTR/L

TRAFFIC LIGHT LINES
A SIMPLIFIED HANDWRITING PROGRAM

iUniverse books may be ordered through booksellers or by contacting:

iUniverse
1663 Liberty Drive
Bloomington, IN 47403
www.iuniverse.com
1-800-Authors (1-800-288-4677)

Because of the dynamic nature of the Internet, any web addresses or links contained in this book may have changed since publication and may no longer be valid. The views expressed in this work are solely those of the author and do not necessarily reflect the views of the publisher, and the publisher hereby disclaims any responsibility for them.

Any people depicted in stock imagery provided by Thinkstock are models, and such images are being used for illustrative purposes only. Certain stock imagery © Thinkstock.

ISBN: 978-1-4917-8568-3 (sc)
ISBN: 978-1-4917-8567-6 (e)

Library of Congress Control Number: 2015921128

Print information available on the last page.

iUniverse rev. date: 01/25/2016

CONTENTS

BACKGROUND STUFF

As with all activities involving children, please provide appropriate supervision when conducting exercises and tasks. All exercises and activities should be completed in a safe environment. Do not attempt any task that is not within your child's capabilities. Please consult a professional with any questions, especially if your child is already receiving occupational therapy services.

Please note that the author of this handwriting program, Kimberly Lane—okay, I'm switching to first person. Third person sounds so formal. I, Kimberly Lane, am an occupational therapist who believes very strongly in the sensory-processing approach to learning. I will, therefore, be very detailed and repetitive and, at times, will try to be funny, particularly because I know that the brain will begin to tune out anything that is too familiar or too unfamiliar, too easy, too complex, too lengthy (requiring you to sit for too long), too boring, or too unrelevant. Don't panic. I know the word is *irrelevant* (I also have a degree in English education); however, I refuse to apply the definition of irrelevant to handwriting, because handwriting is germane and pertinent. It is one of the ways we communicate and a primary mode for our teachers to assess what we know. It is also—for some—hard.

So, back to the tuning-out concern—the brain/nervous system has a remarkable ability to habituate (the neurological term recognizing when an organism ceases to respond to a stimulus). Though I am using the term *habituate* loosely, if the information that you are attending to isn't relevant to your interests, it is likely to be tuned out; you will stop responding to it at some point. Therefore, *unrelevant* feels more appropriate because handwriting applies to most of us (it is germane), but is it in our lineup of things we want to read about? Probably not. So, since I think you are going to tune out from time to time while reading this (you will think of your grocery list, what's on TV tonight, "squirrel," etc.), I am going to repeat some material so that it has a chance to be captured.

Moreover, for you overachievers who won't tune out, even though the brain can tune out too much of some things, it still tends to learn best with repetition. Brains are quirky that way. Hope you didn't tune out through all of that. FYI—the above section was really a plug for sensory processing, particularly sensory modulation—my next book, perhaps. Stayed tuned.

This handwriting program really starts with preschool-level students and runs through to print/manuscript-level writing students, about second grade, developmentally. However, I have not allocated time frames to this program. You will not see sections that say, "This section is for kindergartners." I would like you to approach this with a developmental backdrop, so therefore use the typical age-expected skills as your guide. Each grade can address its traditional role, where preschool should really address the pre-writing skills necessary and kindergarten begins letter formation, and so forth. However, if your older student isn't holding his pencil with an adequate grasp, go to the section that addresses that. If your preschooler already has the prerequisites for handwriting, go ahead and address letter formation. But bear in mind—I strongly believe that we shouldn't leave an area undeveloped or even underdeveloped and move on to the next phase. I know that current curricula require us to move at a very rapid pace. We unfortunately have often been forced to *move on* whether or not our students have *gotten it*. Nonetheless, I see handwriting as the underlayment to learning—meaning we need it to be a solid foundation, one that provides leveling and adhesion. Accordingly, I hope that we plug all the holes and strengthen all the weaknesses of each student's graphomotor skills, affording our students an even playing field. If you take that into account, then all of your students' energy and attention go to the academics and not to the task of handwriting, allowing them to completely concentrate on the subject matter at hand.

I have purposely made this a short program because, well, for one, I believe that it does not need to be long and drawn out. Additionally, though, I would like you to read it through in its entirety, and since I know how busy we all are these days, I needed it to be manageable for you to fit it into your busy schedule and, of course, to not be tuned out. Only then can you see where your student who is struggling with writing might have a weak link.

Once your students have the prerequisites to handwriting (pre-K teachers, we are counting on you for this), then I see the need for about eight weeks, for maybe a half hour a day of instruction, to address all letters. Traditionally, this would be for kindergarten teachers. The final component that I have addressed is targeting and spacing on the Traffic Light Lines. This, however, is incorporated right at the beginning, so, again, it is an area traditionally to be developed from kindergarten through second grade, but for this program, pre-K teachers incorporate it too. If the Traffic Light Lines are used from the beginning, targeting, alignment, and spacing develop naturally and faster. Likewise, for the student who is struggling with alignment in second grade or higher, the Traffic Light Lines help, so go back and use it temporarily until your student integrates the visual-spatial organization for legible writing. Follow this with continual, consistent reinforcement of the rules of writing, and we should have students who can write legibly.

All that is required for this handwriting program is this book, lined paper, three crayons (red, yellow, and green), and a writing tool. Premade worksheets and Traffic Light Line paper are available at TrafficLightLines.com.

Happy writing.

Chapter 1

A QUICK OVERVIEW

As you will see shortly, this handwriting program has grouped all 52 letters into only 7 groups: **The Sticks, The Silly C, The Down, Up and Overs, The Down, Up and Arounds, The Sticks with Kicks, The Kickers**, and finally, **The Stick Arounds.** Each group basically have the same motor pattern or more precisely "motor plan." Grouping letters into as few motor plans as possible allows for easy recall. Students will learn the group's motor plan and then the subtle differences among each letter. If you teach letters individually rather than in groups, then kids need to learn fifty-two motor plans, one for each uppercase and lowercase letter of the alphabet. Fifty-two or seven—what would you rather do?

The above groups of letters are taught on Traffic Light Lines. To make your own Traffic Light lines, take any paper and highlight three lines: red, yellow and green.

_____

_____

_____

Or when appropriate (and capable) have your students highlight the lines of their paper the colors of a traffic light. I recommend using crayons in the beginning because it becomes a tactile barrier. This may become tiresome after a while, so photocopy your work or go to Trafficlightlines.com for premade paper. Please be aware that on the premade paper there is a traffic light in the upper left-hand corner of the paper to help students orient properly. This begins to instill the left-to-right, top-to-bottom orientation for reading and writing. When making your own traffic light lined paper, put a symbol on your paper for this as well. Be sure to allow age-appropriate size for your lines.

Handwriting is initially a visual motor task, meaning the eyes and hand(s) need to work together to form and align letters. Handwriting, however, eventually becomes a kinesthetic task, meaning the proprioceptors (sensory receptors of joints, muscles and tendons) of the hand/arm take on a big part of writing. Our eyes will keep us "in line," but these proprioceptors will drive the ship. Proficient writers can draw any letter in the air or on paper with their eyes closed. Aligning is the challenge and, again, a job for the eyes. To progress your child's kinesthetic ability to write and advance her visual motor planning, practice writing in different media. Resistive media, especially, gives these proprioceptors a lot of feedback. Be creative; use pudding, shampoo, mashed potatoes, shaving cream, putty, clay, and so on. You can draw in these media and even form letters with some of them.

As an occupational therapist, I have steadfastly recommended that people choose one goal to work on at a time when introducing new skills. I say this because often there is more than one goal or motor component or concept embedded in a skill. The brain (or more precisely, the nervous system) needs to focus on the one thing being taught. So, it is going to appear that I am contradicting myself now. Even though I do believe that students should practice letter formation irrespective of the space—meaning without being expected to write on lines because learning the motor plan of the letters is one goal, but aligning letters on the lines is another, this handwriting program recommends teaching the letters on the Traffic Light Lines from the beginning. The reason for this is simple but extremely important: **the Traffic Light Lines help with the motor planning**. Opportunities to write letters not on the Traffic Light Lines are needed so that students have the freedom to expend all their energy on the goal of forming the letters and not sharing that energy and attention with the goal of aligning the letters. So, by all means, create and insert these opportunities into your lessons. But again, the Traffic Light Lines help with the motor planning of forming letters, so in this case, please use the Traffic Light Lines initially as well as writing on unlined paper or in different media, preferably in sensory-based media (finger paint, shaving cream, sand, etc.).

Most of us who have children can share similar stories about how our kids have known about traffic lights since they were two years old because as soon as they saw the light change to green, they were shouting "Go!" from their car seats to the driver who took more than .0001 second to go when the light turned green. Well, that was some of the thinking behind this handwriting program. Kiddos can envision a traffic light. If you have incorporated the Traffic Light Lines from the beginning, even when they aren't using the lines, they will envision them. When they are practicing their letters in other media or on unlined paper, be sure to cue them with their traffic light starts and stops. This, as mentioned, helps with the recall of how to form the letters.

Writing on the Traffic Light Lines will also begin the subsequent processes of handwriting: alignment-eye-hand coordination, spacing, targeting, sizing, and so forth. When they are beginners, however, please do not focus on their difficulty of staying in the lines, as this is a skill that comes as they progress and shouldn't be expected in the beginning.

As just mentioned, this handwriting program has broken down the alphabet (uppercase and lowercase) into just seven groups or "motor plans." Motor planning, by the way, means having an idea of a novel or unfamiliar task or action, developing a plan/strategy for that task or action, and executing that task or action. Any/every task or action really requires motor planning when it is a novel or unfamiliar task or action. Motor planning's big name is praxis. So the way this program works is once you introduce the motor plan of a group, then the Traffic Light Lines assist in differentiating each letter in the group—often, where the letter begins or ends is what differentiates it. For example, *h* and *n* are only different by which "light" the letter begins at. Therefore, *h* is a red light starter (and should be colored red when teaching it, for the additional cue), and *n* is a yellow light starter and should be colored yellow. They both have the same motor plan, which is *down, up, and over*. I am sure you can start to see how I would explain the next letter in the *down, up, and over* group: r. Yes, you are right. Lowercase letter r starts at the yellow light (colored yellow); it is a *down, up, and over,* and it stops at the yellow light. I always go back and contrast a closely linked letter. So I would say, "Unlike *n*, who also starts at the yellow light, it goes down, up, and over but stops at the green light." Compare and contrast as often as possible.

This is therefore the theme of this handwriting program: teach the motor plan for each of the 7 groups of letters, so just seven patterns. You do this using the Traffic Light Lines to direct the letter pattern for starts and stops. Again, the letter group has one motor plan per group. It is the lights (red, yellow, or green) that show the distinction among the letters. For example, P and D are the same except that P ends at the yellow light and D ends at the green. This letter group is the Down, Up, and Around—stick down from the red to the green, back to the red, and go around to the yellow for P and around to the green for D. Once you teach the motor plan for the Down, Up, and Arounds, you will have covered the motor plan for 5 letters, and that is one of the smaller groups. Seven motor plans for 52 letters, that's it. Okay, so here we go.

Chapter 2

Getting Started—Prehension

Prehension Development
Grasps (a.k.a. Prehension)

Handwriting can be directly affected by a person's prehension/grasp on his writing tool. A mature grasp exhibits movement at the fingers, preferably three digits—thumb, index, and middle finger—rather than movement at the wrist, elbow, and/or shoulder. When the movement of the writing tool occurs at the finger level, it is called *dynamic*. A four-digit grasp can also be effective as long as it, too, is dynamic (fingers are the ones moving, not wrist, elbow, or shoulder). When the fingers are still/immobile, but the writing tool is moving, the movement is occurring at the wrist, elbow, or shoulder. This is called a *static* grasp. The farther away from the fingers the movement is occurring, the larger the writing will be. Though static grasps are needed for larger writing or drawing, such as poster work, they directly impede size and precision for general writing tasks.

When it comes to writing (and other manual dexterity tasks), we want the hand to be separated into two sides: thumb, index, and middle finger (or digits one to three) versus ring finger and pinky (digits four and five). The thumb, index, and middle fingers are generally for precision or dexterity. I like to call these the **dexterity digits**. The ring finger and pinky are generally for stabilizing, and even though durability digits is much more clever (cleverer?), I refer to these as **anchor digits**. So, with the separation of the sides of the hand, we are looking for stability power versus precision power. Tucking the anchor digits against the palm (kind of fisted) affords the dexterity digits a stable point to work off of. Therefore, a typical mature tripod grasp will have the dexterity digits on the pencil with the anchor digits supporting them. If the ring finger is also on the pencil (quadrupod), it is usually divided between stability and precision, doing double duty; however, this is also a mature pattern and, therefore, can be very functional.

In order to obtain a mature grasp (i.e., dynamic tripod or dynamic quadrupod), complete activities that support and develop the musculature of the hand as often as possible. Some suggestions are listed below. Furthermore, about twenty degrees of wrist extension is preferable when writing. Slightly inclined surfaces really help facilitate this, such as placing a two-inch binder sideways in front of the child and clipping his paper to it. Having him write on this incline promotes wrist extension and forearm stabilization, and also provides a targeted visual field for attention.

Suggested Activities

Have your student do the following: use tongs to pick up big and little things, cut a lot, manipulate squeeze toys, play with squirt bottles and squirt toys, use trigger tongs (the toy with an animal on the end of a stick that will pick up things with its mouth when you squeeze the trigger on the other end of the stick), color with very small crayons, play with pegs/pegboards, play with Lite-Brite, put coins in a bank, cut a lot—oh, did I mention *cut a lot*? Cut straws (the pieces will fly off); cut Play-Doh; cut and play with putty; and cut and tear cardboard, old holiday cards, invitations, and so forth. Cut a lot. Picking up and placing small objects into anything is an essential concept here, and, of course, cut a lot. Any derivation of this is good, especially with a resistive component (e.g., coins in putty and cutting putty). Palmar arches can be developed with ball play and my personal favorite: take a clean laundry cap and have your child rotate it around with his or her fingers. I usually draw a happy face on it and have the child rotate it around until he or she sees it again.

When doing the above activities, try to use consistent terminology for isolating the thumb and index finger, using them in a pincer motion (or thumb, index, and middle finger). I like to say, "Use your *chompers*," and I demonstrate the thumb and index finger chomping to pick up small objects. As your students get a little more adept, you can place a small object (cotton ball, coin, small toy) in their hands to be held in by the fourth and fifth digits (pressing against the palm). This will really promote that separation of the two sides of the hand: stability power versus precision power.

This chomper concept is then carried over to the next phase, which is picking up and holding their pencils with good prehension (chapter 3).

Draw on a vertical surface as often as possible. This will help with the twenty degrees of wrist extension that is preferable when writing while also strengthening the shoulder girdle. The shoulder girdle is the proximal point between your trunk/core (your stable part) and distal (arm, hand, fingers)—mobile parts. The shoulder girdle needs to be strong to be a stable point for the mobile parts to work off of.

Other activities for shoulder girdle strengthening include the following:

- crawling/playing on all fours
- wheelbarrow walking
- crab walking
- commando crawl
- chair push-ups
- wall push-ups
- playground climbing
- wall ball—rolling a ball up and down a wall (If you have a large white board or chalkboard, have the child draw a maze or road or line to roll the ball along.)

Complete any kid-friendly activity where the shoulder is included—essentially, especially when co-contraction of the musculature is occurring (the muscles around the shoulder—front and back, agonist/antagonist—are involved).

Chapter 3

How to Get Your Kiddos to Hold the Pencil Correctly

To facilitate a mature grasp on writing implements (a.k.a. prehension), do the following:

Step 1. Say to your student, "Place your pencil on the table in front of you, pointing the tip toward the hand doing the writing." (Having the pencil a little toward the center of the student so that it diagonally points to the hand doing the writing, which helps ensure the student will pick it up with the neutral forearm rotation needed.)

Step 2. Say, "Pick it up close to the tip with your chompers" (i.e., thumb and index finger). "Push the pencil top back into the *thumb pocket*" (i.e., the thumb web space). The other fingers will come out to support the writing implement as the child begins to color/draw, especially when writing on a vertical surface.

To develop a mature grasping pattern, continually follow the steps listed above. Be sure that the child is not pronating his forearm (thumb points down). Rather, the forearm should be in neutral-to-supinated (thumb points up) when he is getting in the chomper position for pick up. Be playful, especially for those students who perpetually want to avoid coloring, drawing, and writing.

For students who haven't established a hand dominance yet, be sure to place writing implements on the table in front of them, directly in the center of their bodies (their midline), so that you aren't swaying them to one side or the other. Children who are establishing their dominance should begin to reach out for the marker with their proficient side.

When students continue to switch hands, and there doesn't seem to be an issue with crossing the midline of their bodies, then I will sometimes ask the child to stand in front of me with his eyes closed. Then I say, "On the count of three, open your eyes and grab your marker from me." Usually I am moving the marker toward them as they open their eyes, and often a dominant hand comes out to grab it. I check this a couple of times for consistency. If they continue to switch hands, you could check to see which hand seems more proficient at other tasks and drawing and encourage that side while discouraging the other side, but you may need to consult an OT on this issue.

Chapter 4

UPPERCASE VERSUS LOWERCASE

Even though there is still some debate amongst occupational therapists (OTs) about which case, upper or lower, should come first developmentally, OTs are aware of the pressure on teachers to get children writing. This handwriting program recommends working on the letter formation prerequisites first, as they, after all, are prerequisites. The designs listed below are the handwriting prerequisites. Once a child has mastered these, this program has taken the approach of teaching both uppercase and lowercase letters simultaneously. It seems that most OTs and teachers feel that uppercase is more appropriate to come first developmentally, but the sheer magnitude of lowercase letter writing we do tends to elevate the importance of learning lowercase letters.

Please keep in mind that you need to teach/stress the concept that there are two cases—two ways of writing the same letter. Do not assume that your students realize that the uppercase and its corresponding lowercase letter are the same letter. Many kiddos take a while to make that connection, so continue to reinforce this concept. Be sure to also make mention of the different styles/fonts they may encounter. For example, the "a" in this book (as I sit here typing on my laptop, I realize this) is different from what many of us teach.

Activities to support this would be matching games/tasks with uppercase and lowercase letters. Separate the activities into groups where the uppercase letters that are shaped the same as lowercase but only bigger is one group versus another group where the lowercase letters are completely different from their uppercase counterparts. For example, *C* and *c*, *O* and *o*, versus *A* and *a*, *G* and *g*. This type of activity highlights through contrast.

Another not-so-shameless plug for sensory processing is this: teaching by comparing and contrasting assists kiddos with sensory discrimination difficulties. The details that we naturally discern and therefore take for granted are often lost on children with visual discrimination weakness. So what is obviously a *b* and not a *p* to us might be confusing for a student who struggles with discrimination because the differences are actually quite subtle. Contrast them, particularly by their starting lights (and color) to emphasize their differences. When you are thinking about what I have just said, don't think about our alphabet. Instead, think about Chinese symbols and then check how easily it would be to confuse symbols that you are in the beginning phase of learning, like our kiddos.

Chapter 5

Letter Formation Prerequisites

All letters can be made from the following shapes: vertical line, horizontal line, circle, cross, square, triangle. Using the directionality and language listed below will echo the instructions for the letter formation to be taught later. Always try to be singsongy or add a melody. This helps with motor plan retrieval/recall.

Use props to demonstrate the shapes above: sticks, rulers, your body, doughnuts (eat half to demonstrate the semicircle—for laughs and because doughnuts are delicious), use your own body—kick your foot forward and backward to demonstrate the diagonal line of the Kicker group. Though I just mentioned this point, what is crucial to understand is that all of these prerequisite shapes and the language that is used to teach them transition right to the letter group that they develop. For example, the triangle is the basis for the letter group **Sticks and Kicks—it has a kick back, kick forward, and stick across (forward slash, back slash, horizontal line).** This group has the following letters in it: A, K, k, M, N, Y, Z, z. Add in funny and unexpected props that assist with this (e.g., actual sticks that your kiddos found outside). Use a Barbie doll and kick one of her legs out. If you are really ambitious, have Barbie stand sideways, kick one foot out, and lift one arm out at about 120 degrees, so that she looks like the letter K. Point out the vertical and diagonal lines, and label them as "sticks" and "kicks."

Especially try to contrast a vertical line and diagonal line next to each other. Children are developing their visual-spatial organization over these years, so what looks straight to them often looks crooked/diagonal to us. They need sharp contrasts/extremes to start to assemble this information—true vertical and true horizontal.

Vertical line: |	TEACH THIS AS STICK DOWN
Horizontal line: —	TEACH THIS AS STICK ACROSS
Circle: o	TEACH THIS AS C YOU AROUND.
Cross: +	TEACH THIS AS STICK DOWN, STICK ACROSS
Square/rectangle: ☐	STICK DOWN, STICK ACROSS, STICK UP, STICK ACROSS
Triangle: Δ	KICK BACK, KICK FORWARD, STICK ACROSS

So, again, within these shapes are the components needed for letter formation. Some of the motions are buried, though, such as

1) Diagonal lines (a.k.a. obliques) are in the triangle. Refer to diagonal lines as *kicks*. You can demonstrate this by standing sideways. Tell your kiddos that your body is a *stick* that goes straight up and down. Then kick your foot in front of you as though you just kicked a ball and hold it there. Then show your students that this diagonal pattern with your leg is a kick—kick forward and kick back. Some of our letter groups will be referred to as *sticks* (such as l, t), *kicks* (such as w), and *sticks with kicks* (such as k).

2) Semicircles are in the circle. You can refer to these as the front half of a circle and the back half of a circle, or a C. This is where eating half of a doughnut is helpful. I think maybe there aren't any calories when you are using food props to teach children. So go ahead and take one for the team. Also, use this opportunity to show the difference between an awake C and a sleepy C (otherwise known as a U). We need our kiddos to start the letter C in the right spot so that it can make all the other letters in the Awake C group.

Practice the above-mentioned shapes as often as possible in a variety of media as well as on the practice worksheets in accordance with the student's skill level.

Chapter 6

INSTRUCTIONS FOR PREREQUISITE SHAPES

You can work on each of these shapes separately, in or on any media. They are best addressed, though, when drawn onto Traffic Light Lines, so the colors help with the directionality and motor plan as well as introducing the letter groups that derive from each shape. I like to have a design drawn for students to trace, then a design with dashed lines for tracing, fading to just dots for cues, and eventually having them draw independently. Worksheets are available at **Trafficlightlines.com**. Once you have sufficiently demonstrated the motion, be sure to use the boldface verbiage listed at the end of each design. Have your student say it as well.

Beginner

Vertical—refer to these lines as sticks, as this is the prerequisite design for the sticks letter group. Start at the red line and stick down to the green and also start at the yellow light and stick down to the green. Say, "STICK DOWN." (For future reference, The Sticks group has E, F, H, i, I, l, L, t, T.)

Horizontal—refer to these lines as sticks. Start at the red, yellow, and green line and stick across. Say, "STICK ACROSS."

Circle—try to point out the C motion, as this is a big group of letters later. I use the verbiage, "C YOU AROUND." Make a point of having the two points touch. I say, "Give a high five," or "Make them hold hands," or "Give it a kiss," with a big kiss sound when the two points come together. Start at the red line and go to the left. Also, practice starting at the yellow light and go to the left with "C you around" verbiage.

Intermediate

Cross—again, these are sticks. Start at the red line, stick down to the green, and cross at the yellow. Say, "STICK DOWN, STICK ACROSS."

Square—though a square can be drawn with segmented lines, it is more efficient to facilitate four contiguous lines, as this is needed for letter formation (for example, uppercase L). Starting at the red light, stick down to the green, stick across at the green, stick up to the red, and stick across at the red. Remind your kiddos to stick up to the *same height* as the stick down; otherwise, you get a triangle or rounded corners. Say, "STICK DOWN, STICK ACROSS, STICK UP, STICK ACROSS."

Triangle—this shape is the prerequisite to the *sticks with kicks* group. For those who do not have directionality yet, starting at the red light, say, "Kick back to the green light (left). Go back to the red. Kick forward to the green light (right). Stick across at the green." Say, "KICK BACK, KICK FORWARD, STICK ACROSS."

Advanced

Right oblique (forward slash)—starting at the red light, kick back to the green. Say, "KICK BACK." These should also be practiced starting at the yellow light. This design is a prerequisite is for the letter group *kickers*.

Left oblique (backslash)—starting at the red light, kick forward to the green light. Say, "KICK FORWARD." These should also be practiced starting at the yellow light (*kickers* letter group).

X—same as above. This design is for the kickers letter group. Say, "Kick forward, kick back." Start at the red light, kick forward to the green light, back to the red light, and kick back to the green light. Say, "KICK FORWARD, KICK BACK." Practice this starting at the yellow light to the green also.

C (left semicircle)—ambitious overachievers can begin to introduce the Awake C group here. Start at the top or red line and go around to the left, down to the green light. I sometimes refer to this as the back half of a circle. You know your kiddos;

use what works. Don't forget the doughnuts. This one should also be practiced starting at the yellow light. Say, "C YOU AROUND." Practice this at the yellow light to the green as well (lowercase c).

U—this shape is the introduction to the *stick around* group. Starting at the red light, stick down to the green light, go around, and stick up to the red light. For this one, you say, "Stick down, around, stick up." This one should also be practiced starting at the yellow light. Point out the difference here between Awake C and this sleepy looking C.

Right semicircle—start at the red light, go around to the right, stop at the green light. This shape is the front half of a circle (or the other half to your doughnut). It is essential for the letters in the Down, Up, and Around group. Say, "AROUND." The contrast here is that the left semicircle goes to the left to begin the C orientation—remark on the difference between C You Around and Around. Practice this shape at the yellow light as well.

Again, drawing directly on the Traffic Light Lines provides color cues for directionality and motor planning as well as opportunity to connect to the letters that these shapes produce. However, they can and should be drawn anywhere. Try to add in the traffic light color cues when not using the traffic light lines.

Practice these designs repeatedly. Incorporate these shapes into activities and crafts, drawing them and cutting them. Draw them in, and cut them out of different media, such as sand, shaving cream, Play-Doh, putty, old cards, card stock, sandpaper, tinfoil, and so on. Cutting is important because it develops the separation of the sides of the hand, as mentioned earlier. Again, this is important because it affords children more mature grasping patterns on writing utensils, and this is important because weak or immature grasps on writing tools will impede precision, mobility, and speed, therefore negatively affecting a child's handwriting.

Be sure to pay attention to your student's position. Static grasps are okay in the beginning, meaning that the child is writing with movement of the marker occurring at the shoulder, elbow, or wrist. However, the goal is to have the movement occurring at the digits/fingers (dynamic grasp). If the movement is occurring at joints far away from the fingers, the writing will be large. The farther away it is from the fingers, the larger the drawing/writing will be.

Once proficient with the prerequisite designs, students are ready to begin uppercase and lowercase letter formation. Though this program encourages students to write in a variety of media (sand, Play-Doh, shaving cream, etc.), it is strongly recommended to practice on Traffic Light Lines. Direction matters. Incorrect starting points and inaccurate directions cause challenges with sizing and spacing later on, when students are writing words and sentences.

Chapter 7

Uppercase and Lowercase Letters

Rules to Reinforce

All uppercase letters start at the red light and touch the green light. Not one uppercase letter goes below the green light, and no uppercase letter starts anywhere else. In this case, we say, "All uppercase letters stay in between the red and the green."

As mentioned, when teaching the letters, it is recommended that you color the letter you are teaching the same color as the light in which it starts. So if it's tall, color it red, and if it's small, color it yellow. The only exceptions are lowercase d and the Five That Drive through the Green Light. Lowercase d starts at the yellow light because it is a lowercase c first, and therefore it is colored yellow. The Five That Drive through the Green Light (g, j, p, q, y) aren't exactly small, but they certainly aren't tall. The Five that Drive through the Green light are, as their name implies, the only five letters that go below the green light. They all, however, start at the yellow light and should be colored yellow. I have, at times, colored them green to differentiate that they go below the green light, but this can be confusing for some since the color of the letter indicates where it starts, and no letter starts at the green light. Use your own discretion on this.

As mentioned earlier, occupational therapists, in particular, struggle with which letter case should be taught first. Since we capitalize only the first letter of the first word of every sentence and proper nouns, most letters/words are lowercase. The majority of our letters are lowercase. Therefore, students need to learn them right away and practice them often.

I included the above paragraph to drive the following point home. In the above paragraph alone, there are 301 letters—only four of them are uppercase. Students need to practice lowercase letters.

As mentioned before, all uppercase letters start at the red light and go to the green, so no uppercase letter starts at the yellow light. However, for lowercase letters, the middle line (a.k.a. the yellow light) is particularly important.

Why is the middle line / yellow light important? **Because 20 lowercase letters start at the middle line. That is 77 percent of the letters in our lowercase alphabet.** Whether it is drawn on the paper or not, students need to know the middle line. Having said that, I recommend that the middle line is drawn in, at least for beginners.

In the above paragraph, there are 263 lowercase letters. Guess how many of them started at the yellow light. I think it was 196. If I'm right then that was 75 percent of that paragraph. **Teach the middle line**.

Chapter 8

LETTER GROUPS

As mentioned, I have divided the letters of the alphabet into seven groups, so you can plan your time for teaching handwriting in these chunks. (You will see eight below. Each of the letters in the eighth group are found in the other seven groups. Those letters have been grouped together additionally to highlight another commonality.)

I recommend spending at least one week per group. Focus on each group's category. For example, "The down, up, and overs" means the motion is going to be down, up, and over … funny how that works. When you reinforce the same motor plan for a set of letters, you expedite the recall of how to initiate the letter. Then the student only needs to address the subtle differences. For example, the down, up, and over letters *h* and *n* are simply different due to where you start, at the red light or the yellow light.

Reinforce that the letters are colored the same as the light they start at. I think I have heard that before; just checking on whether you tuned out or not.

The letter groups are as follows:

1) **Silly C (made up of two subgroups: Awake C and C You Arounds)**

2) **Down, Up, and Over**

3) **Down, Up, and Around**

4) **Sticks**

5) **Sticks with Kicks**

6) **Kickers**

7) **Stick Arounds**

8) The **Five That Drive** through the green light

The last group of letters (eight) is already included in one of the other above groups but additionally form their own group because they are the only letters allowed to go past the green light. Their motor plans do not need to be re-taught as, again, they have been included in other groups, but the rule that instructs them to drive through the green light does. See below.

The Silly C: Awake C and C You Arounds

Awake C:

Lowercase	Uppercase
c, o, a, d, g, q	C, G (with sticks), O, Q (with a kick)

C You Around:

Lowercase	Uppercase
s (I sometimes teach e here)	S

Stick Around

Lowercase	Uppercase
e, f, j, u	J, U

Down, Up and Overs

Lowercase	Uppercase
h, n, r, m	

Down, Up, and Arounds

Lowercase	Uppercase
b, p	B, P, D, R (with a kick)

Sticks

Lowercase	Uppercase
i, l, t	E, F, H, I, L, T

Sticks with Kicks

Lowercase	Uppercase
k, z	A, K, M, N, Y, Z

Kickers

Lowercase	Uppercase
v, w, x, y	V, W, X

The Five That Drive through the green light

Lowercase	Uppercase
g, j, p, q, y	

The *five that drive* letters all fall into other groups (Awake C, Kickers, etc.); however, they are unique in that they are the *only* letters that go past the green light. So they form their own group. These letters all start at the yellow light. Remind students that it is okay to go into the space below the green light for this group of letters. Many students think they are coloring outside the lines, so to speak, with the driving letters and instead will try to squeeze them into the space above the green light. Highlight that it is okay and actually required to drive through the green light for these five letters. Again, remind them that they are *all* yellow light starters. If you are feeling ambitious, try to make the connection that since they are all yellow light starters, they must be all lowercase letters since **all uppercase letters start at the red light and stay in between the red and the green.** Further, you should remind them that these are the only letters to drive through the green light by saying, "**All the rest stay in between the red and the green.**" Okay, let's get on with the letters.

Chapter 9

TEACHING LETTER FORMATION

Again, the letters are taught on the Traffic Light Lines. So have your paper colored red (top line), yellow (middle line), and green (bottom line). The directions below talk you through the motion. When teaching each letter group, be sure to have the letters colored the same color of the light at which they start. Letters that start at the red light (top line) are colored red. Letters that start at the yellow light (middle line) are colored yellow. **No letters start at the green light (bottom line); therefore, no letters are colored green. Also, all uppercase letters start at the red light; therefore, they are all colored red.**

Once your students learn a group, play the following game if time allows. Say, "I'm thinking of a letter that is a down, up, and over. It starts at the red light …" Have them shout out the answer or write it on the board. You can eventually do this for the entire uppercase and lowercase alphabet. It's great for visual memory, auditory memory, and graphomotor skills.

Sticks: E, F, H, i, I, l, L, t, T
The sticks are probably the easiest letters to learn and teach. The language is simple—"stick down and stick across." If your kiddos were taught this program from the prerequisite phase, then they know the *stick down and stick across* motor plan well.

For lowercase letter i:
Instruct students to start at the yellow light and stick down. They can put a circle or dot or dash above it or not; that will come naturally.

For uppercase letter I (that is, I as in ice cream. Sensing a food theme? Don't write on an empty stomach):
Instruct students to start at the red light and stick down to the green. Stick across at the red and stick across at the green.

For lowercase letter l:
Instruct students to start at the red light and stick down to the green.

For uppercase letter L:
Instruct students to start at the red light and stick down and stick across at the green.

For lowercase letter t:
Instruct students to start at the red light, stick down to the green, and stick across at the yellow.

For uppercase letter T:
Instruct students to start at the red light, stick down to the green, and stick across at the red light.

For uppercase letter F:
Instruct students to start at the red light, stick down to the green, stick across at the red light, and stick across at the yellow light.

For uppercase letter E:
Instruct students to start at the red light, stick down to the green, stick across at the red light, stick across at the yellow light, and stick across at the green light.

For uppercase H:
Instruct students to start at the red light and stick down to the green. Instruct them to move over, stick down from red to green again, and stick across at the yellow in between.

The Down, Up, and Overs: h, n, r, and m

The down, up, and overs are fairly simple to teach and learn. They are very similar in most ways, short of where they start and stop. Lowercase m is the only one that goes over one more time. Be sure to start out by explaining that once you go over, you stick down. This will be useful to contrast the down, up, and arounds (the next group to be taught) where once you go over, you go back around.

For lowercase h:

Instruct your students to start at the red light, stick down to the green, and go up and over at the yellow light, straight down to the green. Once you have introduced this, have them repeat the motion while saying, "Down, up, and over."

For lowercase n:

Instruct your students to start at the yellow light, stick down to the green, go up and over at the yellow light, and stick down to the green. Once you have introduced this, have them repeat the motion while saying, "Down, up, and over."

For lowercase r:

Instruct your students to start at the yellow light, stick down to the green, go up and over at the yellow light, and stop. Once you have introduced this, have them repeat the motion while saying, "Down, up, and over."

For lowercase m:

Instruct students to start at the yellow light, stick down to the green, go up and over at the yellow light, stick down to the green and up and over at the yellow again, and finally stick down to the green. Once you have introduced this, have them repeat the motion while saying, "Down, up, and over, up and over."

The Down, Up, and Arounds: b, p, B, D, R (with a kick)

For the down, up, and arounds, you should explain that this group is like the down, up, and overs but that instead of sticking down you go around like the front half of a circle (or half a doughnut), back to the stick you started with. So **the down, up, and arounds go back to the stick you started with.**

For lowercase b:

Instruct your students to start at the red light, stick down to the green, go up and around at the yellow light, and stop back at the green. Once you have introduced this, have them repeat the motion while saying, "Down, up, and around."

For lowercase p:

Instruct your students to start at the yellow light, dive down past the green, go up to the yellow light and around to the green light. "Down, up, and around." You should begin to introduce the **five that drive** at this point if you haven't already. Tell students that p is one of the **five that drive through the green light** and list the others (g, j, p, q, y) even though they haven't been addressed yet.

For uppercase D:

Instruct students to start at the red light, stick down to the green, go up to the red and around to the green. "Down, up, and around." Incorporate the verbiage *back to the stick you started with* when needed.

For uppercase B:

Instruct your students to start at the red light, stick down to the green, go up to the red and back around to the yellow, and around to the green. Once you have introduced this, have them repeat the motion while saying, "Down, up, and around and around."

For uppercase R: (down, up and around with a kick)

Instruct your students to start at the red light, stick down to the green, go up to the red and back around to the yellow, and kick forward to the green. Once you have introduced this, have them repeat the motion while saying, "Down, up, and around, kick forward.

The Silly C Letters: Awake C Group and C You Arounds

This group has the most letters in it, twelve, but has been divided into two groups: Awake C and C You Arounds. If your student went through the prerequisite phase, then he or she should have the letter c down pat. If your student does not have this, then you need to practice it.

Awake C Letters: a, d, g, o, q and, of course, lower and uppercase c, C, G (with sticks), O, and Q (with a kick)

The phrases I use are as follows:
- Awake c can make an *a*.
- Awake c can make a *d*.
- Awake c can make a *g*.
- Awake c can make an *o*.
- Awake c can make a *q*.

All of the lowercase letters in this group start at the middle line; therefore, they are colored yellow. Two of them also drive through the green light. All of the uppercase letters in this group start at the red light. And of course that makes sense since *all* uppercase letters start at the red light.

For lowercase c:
If your students didn't master it in the prerequisite phase, instruct students to start at the yellow light, circle back, and stop at the green light. Say, "c you around."

For uppercase C:
Instruct students to start at the red light, circle back, and stop at the green light. Don't hesitate to compare and contrast, showing that uppercase and lowercase c are only different because of which light they start at.

When students demonstrate competence with the letter c, introduce the Awake C letters—o, O, a, d, g, q, G, and Q in that order. Clarify that their c must be wide awake, sitting upright; otherwise, he is a **sleepy c**, and a sleepy c look like the letter u.

For lowercase letter o:
Remind students that "awake c can make an o." Then instruct students to make a c starting at the yellow light and close it back at the yellow light. *Awake c can make an o.* Practice lowercase o.

For uppercase O:
Same as lowercase o but start at the red light. Point this out to them.

For lowercase a:
Remind students that "awake c can make an a." Then instruct students to make a c starting at the yellow light. Close it at the yellow light and stick down to the green light. Practice the letter a.

For lowercase d:
Remind students that "awake c can make a d." Then instruct students to make a c starting at the yellow light and then go up to the red light and stick down to the green.

For lowercase g:
Remind students that "awake c can make a g." Then instruct students to make a c starting at the yellow light and then close it at the yellow light. Then stick down

29

past the green light, go around, and stick up to the left. *Stick down around, stick up* shows up again in the *stick around* group. Practice the letter g. Remind students that the letter g is also one of the *five that drive through the green light.*

For lowercase q:

Remind students that "awake c can make a q." Then instruct them to make a c starting at the yellow light. Close it at the yellow light, stick down past the green light, go around, and stick up to the right. Practice the letter q. Remind students that the letter q is one of the *five that drive through the green light.*

For uppercase G:

Remind students that "awake C can make uppercase G." Then instruct them to make a C starting at the red light. Then stick up to the yellow and stick across at the yellow.

For uppercase Q:

Remind students that "awake C can make uppercase Q." Instruct students to make a C starting at the red light and close it at the red light. Kick down from the yellow light in the middle of the circle.

C You Arounds: s, S

Truth be told, this group had a lot of other letters in it (e, f, u, j) and went through a variety of names, like sleepy c and lazy c and crazy c and baby c and sticky c groups. I decided to break up the group because solid motor plans are more important than clever labels. So this group is very small because it does not have enough of a common motor plan to be grouped with other letters.

For lowercase s:

Instruct your students to start at the yellow light, make a baby c, and go back around to the green. The mantra here is *baby c you around.*

For uppercase S:

Instruct your students to start at the red light, make a lowercase c or baby c to the yellow light, and go around to the green. Say, "Baby c you around."

Lowercase e is listed below but can fit here too. I like to say, "Stick across and c you around."

Stick Arounds: e, f, j, u, J, U

These letters all have sticks and around motions. The U is practiced in the prerequisite phase, so students should have some proficiency, and there is a c in the e and the beginnings of a C in the f, so use those motor plans to assist.

For lowercase e:

Instruct student to start just below the yellow light and stick across. Then go up and around at the yellow, down to the green. You might want to instruct them to stick across just below the yellow light and make a c at the yellow light. The original name for this group with lowercase e was sticky C. Maybe I should have stuck with that. The mantra after you have introduced it is "stick across and c you around" or "stick across and make a c." However, I prefer "stick across and c you around."

For lowercase f:

Instruct students to start at the red light, go around, and quickly stick down to the green. Around and stick down, cross at the yellow. You might want to point out that you can start making an uppercase C but quickly stick down to the green and stick across at the yellow. So C you around, stick down, stick across.

For lowercase j:

Instruct students to start at the yellow light and stick down. Remind them to drive past the green and go around to the left. Once you have introduced this, have them say, "Stick down, go around, stick up." Remind them that j is one of the five that drive through the green light.

For lowercase u:

Instruct students to start at the yellow light, stick down to the green, go around to the right, and stick up to the yellow, stick down to the geen. Once this has been introduced, you say, "Stick down, around, stick up, stick down."

For uppercase J:

Instruct students to start at the red light, stick down to the green, and go around and stick up to the yellow. "Stick down, go around, stick up."

For uppercase U:

Instruct students to start at the red light, stick down, go around at the green, and stick up to the red. "Stick down, go around, stick up."

Sticks with Kicks: k, z, A, K, M, N, Y, Z

This group has, as the name already tells you, sticks and kicks—that is, vertical and horizontal lines with diagonal lines (a.k.a. obliques).

For lowercase k:

Instruct students to start at the red light, stick down to the green. Go over to the yellow light, and kick back to the stick and kick forward to the green. Once you have introduced this, you say, "Stick down, kick back, kick forward."

For lowercase z:

Instruct students to start at the yellow light, stick across, kick back to the green, and stick across at the green. "Stick across, kick back, stick across."

For uppercase Z:

Instruct your students to do the same as the lower case z but start at the red light. Point out to your students that uppercase and lowercase z are the same except for the light it starts at.

For uppercase A:

Instruct your students to start at the red light, kick back to the green, go back to the red, kick forward to the green, and stick across at the yellow. "Kick back, kick forward, stick across."

For uppercase K:

Instruct your students to start at the red light, stick down to the green, move over to the red light, kick back to the yellow, and kick forward to the green. "Stick down, kick back, kick forward." Show students that uppercase and lowercase k are different only where they start to kick back (red light for uppercase K and yellow for lowercase k).

For uppercase M:

Instruct your students to start at the red light, stick down to the green, go back to the red light, kick forward, kick up to the red, and stick down to the green. "Stick down, kick forward, kick up, stick down."

For uppercase N:

Instruct your students to start at the red light, stick down to the green, go back to the red light, kick forward to the green, and stick up to the red. "Stick down, kick forward, stick up."

For uppercase Y:

Instruct your students to start at the red light, kick forward to the yellow, kick up to the red, go to the yellow point, and stick down to the green. "Kick forward, kick up, stick down."

Kickers: v, w, x, y, V, W, X

For lowercase v:

Instruct your students to start at the yellow light, kick forward to the green light, and kick up to the yellow light. "Kick forward, kick up."

For uppercase V:

Same as above, except start at the red light and end at the red light. "Kick forward, kick up."

For lowercase w:

Instruct your students to start at the yellow light, kick forward to the green, kick up to the yellow, kick forward to the green, and kick up to the yellow. "Kick forward, kick up, kick forward, kick up."

For uppercase W:

Same as above, except start at the red, go back to red, and end at red. "Kick forward, kick up, kick forward, kick up." (Kick up to the yellow or the red—your call.)

For lowercase x:

Instruct your students to start at the yellow, kick forward to the green, move forward to the yellow, and kick back to the green. "Kick forward, kick back."

For uppercase X:

Same as above, except start from the red light, not the yellow. "Kick forward, kick back."

That was all fifty-two letters.

Chapter 10

SPACING

Spacing is the last area to be covered. Spacing between letters and between words is addressed here. We tend to focus on the spacing between words and often guide our students to leave a finger space in between each word. If this is working, do not reinvent the wheel. If it is not working, as I have found that it tends to stop the flow of writing, then read on. Also, we often neglect to address the spacing between the letters of each word, which is more often the issue with students' spacing. Students often do not realize that the letters of each word have spacing rules too. More often than not, students will leave too large of a space between the letters of a word. Due to developing visual-spatial organization as well as newly acquired letter formation, students tend to fear that they are going to bump into the letter they just wrote with the letter they are about to write, and consequently, they move over too far. Stress to your kiddos that closer is usually better and often necessary. Lastly, I have not given instruction as to how to teach indentation and margins because typical and minimal cueing is all that will be necessary as students become proficient with general spacing.

I have divided spacing into two simple concepts: **space sticks** and **space bubbles**. **Space Sticks** are for spacing between the letters of each word and **Space Bubbles** are for the spaces between each word. The rules for spacing go as follows:

1) When letters group together to form a word, they are buddies, and buddies **stick** together, so only a **space stick** should be able to fit between the letters of each word. Draw a line/stick between the letters of the words you are using to

demonstrate. When more than two lines/sticks can be drawn in, it is too large of a space because three space sticks equals a space bubble.

2) There should be enough room between each word so that the words **pop** off the page. A **space bubble** should be able to be drawn in between each word. After they have written a word, have them count "one, two, three" as they slowly glide their hand over to write the next word. Again, lll = O; that is, three space sticks equals a space bubble.

The rules should be repeated often:

The letters of each word are buddies and buddies stick together. Only a space stick should fit between each letter.

Each word needs to pop off the page, so words need to be far enough apart so that a space bubble can be drawn in. A beginner should count "one, two, three" as he or she slowly glides his or her hand over to write the next word in the sentence.

Three space sticks equal a space bubble.

Wow, you made it to the end. Hope you didn't tune out too much. Too much with the tuning-out comments?

Happy writing!